Box splits

Balance in pairs

Ready for training

Performing a walkover

Squat balance

Working with a hoop

THE YOUNG GYMNAST

JOAN JACKMAN

Finishing position

Cartwheeling

Supporting a handstand

Mounting the beam

An arabesque

FOREWORD BY
SHANNON MILLER

V-sit

London • New York • Stuttgart

*Moving into a
shoulder balance*

A DORLING KINDERSLEY BOOK

Project editor Stella Love **Art editor** Lesley Betts

Photography Ray Moller

Picture research Anna Lord

Production Catherine Semark

Deputy editorial director Sophie Mitchell
Deputy art director Miranda Kennedy

The young gymnasts
Nick Addo, Ben Brown, Lucy Carnan, Adam Edwards,
Becky McCormack, Chloe Prangnell, Cheryl Wilcox

First published in Great Britain in 1995 by
Dorling Kindersley Limited
9 Henrietta Street, London WC2E 8PS

A CIP catalogue record for this book is available from the British Library.

ISBN 0 7513 5286 1

Colour reproduction by Colourscan, Singapore
Printed and bound by Arnoldo Mondadori, Verona, Italy

Contents

8
To all young gymnasts

10
Starting gymnastics

12
Gymnastics apparatus

14
Making shapes

16
Rolls and rolling

18
Backward rolls

20
Balances

22
Headstands
and handstands

24
Cartwheels
and round-offs

26
Backflips
and walkovers

28
Jumps and leaps

30
Making a sequence

32
Vaulting

34
The balance beam

36
Rhythmic gymnastics

38
Sports acrobatics

40
Tumbling

42
Competitions

43
Glossary

44
Index

45
Useful addresses
and Acknowledgments

At the World Championships
Shannon Miller with the gold medal she
won when she took the all-around title
at the 1993 World Championships.
At the same event, she also won the
individual apparatus titles for the
asymmetric bars and floor exercises.

To all young gymnasts

"**G**YMNASTICS is much more than a beautiful sport to watch. It also develops your muscles, your sense of balance, and your flexibility. With the improvement in your physical appearance comes a wonderful sense of self-esteem. Whether you just take classes or decide to compete, your mind and your body will benefit from the exercise and discipline required. Competition brings even greater rewards. You learn poise and the ability to control your fears. You get to travel and meet lots of other kids, and you learn to take instruction well. You'll probably find that your schoolwork improves – even though you have less time for homework – because you become much better organized. But most important, training and competing are fun! I know you'll really enjoy reading this book and I hope it will help you to discover and appreciate the exciting world of gymnastics. **"**

Shannon Miller

*"It is so exciting to
travel with your team
to a competition."*

*"If one or more of your scores
counts towards a team trophy,
you feel terrific!"*

*"Each day is a new
adventure in learning, both
mentally and physically."*

History of gymnastics

FROM PAINTINGS, pottery, and other historical evidence we know that forms of gymnastics were practised more than 3,000 years ago in Ancient Egypt and later in Greek and Roman times. As the Roman Empire declined, so too did gymnastics. For many centuries, only wandering entertainers kept acrobatic and juggling skills alive. Then, early in the 19th century, two men – F. Jahn of Germany and P. Ling of Sweden – introduced new ways to exercise, from which modern gymnastics developed.

Swinging rings was an Olympic event for women.

Acrobatic entertainers
At the end of the 17th century, acrobats often performed during the interval of a play.

A gymnasium in 1859
Here you can see some early forms of apparatus used today, such as the vaulting horse, which was shaped like a real horse until 1930. Many of the exercises in progress are to develop arm and shoulder strength.

Rings

Wall bars are still seen in many gyms today.

Clubs and dumb-bells

Parallel bars

A girls' school gymnasium in 1900
Clubs and dumbbells were used to develop strength and suppleness in the arms and shoulders. There were few exercises for the rest of the body.

Gymnastics today

Today, gymnastics and its various disciplines is a popular sport for girls and boys of all ages. You may choose to work in general gymnastics only, learning some skills from all the disciplines, and training just for fun. Or you may decide to specialize in just one of the disciplines shown below.

Holding a balance

Girls' artistic gymnastics
This is a competitive discipline in which you work on your own on each of four pieces of apparatus – the asymmetric bars, the floor, the beam, and the vault.

Making a bridge

Boys' artistic gymnastics
This is a competitive discipline, like girls' artistic gymnastics, but boys work on six pieces of apparatus – floor, pommel horse, rings, parallel bars, horizontal bar, and vault.

Balancing with a partner

Rhythmic gymnastics
This is another discipline for girls. It requires great suppleness and involves many dance movements which are made while working with small hand apparatus – ball, hoop, rope, ribbon, or clubs.

Working with hand apparatus

Sports acrobatics
Boys and girls take part in sports acrobatics. Balances form a major part of this discipline but it also involves other gymnastic skills, such as acrobatics, dance movements, and tumbling.

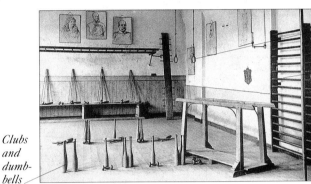

Starting gymnastics

GYMNASTICS IS a very exciting sport. If you have enjoyed gymnastics in school and want to improve, or if you have been thrilled by gymnastics on television, you may feel inspired to join a club and start training. Start by finding out what clubs are available in your area. Think about the sort of gymnastics you would like to try. You will not need any special clothes when you begin. Wearing a T-shirt and shorts will be suitable at first, but eventually you will need to get the sort of clothing shown here. Your coach will advise you when you are ready to buy special equipment such as handguards.

Leotards are named after a French acrobat, Jules Léotard, who was the first person to wear one.

Sleeveless leotard

Girls' clothes

Girls wear leotards. Leotards are made of stretchy fabrics and fit closely. This helps your coach to see the body shapes you make and how you move during practice, so that your mistakes can be corrected. Leotards are ideal for gymnastics because they are comfortable to wear and allow you to move freely.

Leotards are stretchy and close-fitting.

Make sure your clothes are always clean and neat.

Joining a club

Go along to watch a club session before you join. Look to see if the gym is clean and the apparatus in good condition. Try to find out if the coaches are well qualified and ask if the club is a member of the sport's governing organization. Check if you will be able to take gymnastics awards once you are a member, or enter competitions, if this interests you. Then, if you are satisfied, join the club and get started.

Most gymnasts prefer to work in bare feet.

Jewellery
Do not wear watches or jewellery in the gym. They may cause injury and can damage the apparatus.

Boys' clothes

Boys wear shorts over a sleeveless leotard for practice sessions. In competition, they may wear shorts for floorwork and vaulting, but on the other pieces of apparatus boys must wear long trousers.

Keeping warm

You will need a tracksuit or similar clothes to wear during the warm-up and during training if it is very cold.

Tracksuit

Your club may have tracksuits and leotards in the club's own colours.

Boys' and girls' training

In the early stages of training, boys and girls learn many of the same basic skills and use much of the same equipment. Some of the boys' apparatus requires great strength and the boys only begin to specialize when they are older and stronger. Girls have to be strong and supple, too but they can produce simple sequences on their apparatus at a young age.

Ready for training

Pack your kit carefully so that you always arrive at the gym with everything you need.

Hair

Your hair should be neat and tidy, and not falling in your eyes. If you have long hair, tie it back or plait it so that it is off your face and cannot swing to hit either you or your coach.

Boys' handguard

A small metal ridge helps the boys to grip the bars.

Girls' handguards

Handguards

Gymnasts usually wear handguards for work on the bars and rings. Handguards prevent blisters forming and help the swinging and circling movements required.

Chalk

Chalk

Many gymnasts put chalk on their hands and feet. The chalk stops their hands from getting sticky with perspiration and prevents their feet slipping on the mats.

Warming up

Every session will start with a warm-up. This is a series of exercises to make your heart beat faster, increase your breathing rate, loosen your muscles and joints, and make you more supple, preventing stiffness and injury. The warm-up will make you ready to work.

Wrists and fingers do a lot of work. Warm them up well.

There are exercises for every part of you.

Warm-up exercises

The exercises used in the warm-up should include every part of your body. You will be able to practise some of them at home, which will help to make you supple and strong.

Bend, stretch, shake, and circle your feet and ankles.

Gymnastics apparatus

APPARATUS FOR artistic gymnastics has changed greatly over the years. In the early days there were no set measurements for the equipment. Then, almost 50 years ago, rules were agreed about the apparatus to be used in Olympic and World championships. Since then, the apparatus has been constantly improved and updated. The new materials used, and advances in training, have helped to make possible the spectacular gymnastics you see today. You may see some of this apparatus in your gym, but before you will be able to start using it, you will have to master some basic skills, and improve your strength, stamina, and suppleness.

Rings
Rings are used only in men's gymnastics but until 40 years ago women used them, too. Modern rings are 18 cm in diameter and hang 275 cm above the floor. Here, Travis Romagnoli of Canada shows the strength and control needed for work on the rings.

Scoreboard

Asymmetric bars

Vault run-up

Pommel horse
The pommel horse is 160 cm long and stands 120 cm high. It is used only for the pommel exercise in men's gymnastics. Here you can see Vitaly Marinich of Ukraine in action. He travels along the horse, supported on his hands, as he makes smooth, swinging movements with his legs and body.

Parallel bars
The parallel bars are part of the men's apparatus. The gymnast has to travel above and between the wooden bars, on his hands, upper arms, or on one arm, as in this Diamidov turn shown by Andrei Kan of Belarus.

Vaulting horse
The vaulting horse is used by men and women. It is 160 cm long, 35 cm wide, and its height is adjustable. The top is slightly padded, and covered in suede or another non-slip material.

Women use the horse at a height of 120 cm, and men at 135 cm.

Balance beam
A beam exercise lasts between 70 and 90 seconds. It is performed only by women. The beam is 500 cm long but only 13 cm wide. Its height is adjustable, but for competitions it is set at 120 cm. The surface of the beam is padded to make it slightly springy. This helps to cushion the gymnasts as they land on it.

Floor

Floor exercises take place on a carpeted area 12 metres square, which is built on a springy base. The edge of the area is marked by a white line and surrounded by a wide, sloping, safety border.

Beam *Parallel bars*

Floor

Vaulting horse

Competition arena

This arena is set out for a major artistic gymnastics competition. Each piece of apparatus is surrounded by safety mats. Tables for the judges are placed where the judges will have a clear view. The judges enter the scores for each exercise into an electronic score box and the scores are relayed to a central computer.

Rings

Chalk bucket

Score box

Safety mat

Asymmetric bars

Fan Di of China shows a popular mount on the asymmetric bars. These bars are used only in women's work. An exercise should include swings, circles, and handstand positions. An advanced gymnast will include release and catch moves – letting go of the bar, performing a move in the air, then catching the bar again.

Horizontal bar

Valeri Liukin of Ukraine performs on the horizontal bar. The bar is 240 cm wide, and used only by men. It is set at 275 cm from the floor, and to start an exercise, the gymnast's coach will lift him up. Much of the work is similar to the women's work on the asymmetric bars and includes spectacular circles around the bar, and release and catch moves.

Springboard

A springboard is a device that helps you to rebound upwards. It is used for vaulting, and for mounting other apparatus, such as the beam and asymmetric bars. It is 120 cm long, and rises about 20 cm from the floor.

You can adjust the height of most apparatus.

Making shapes

THE SHAPES you can make with your body are the essence of gymnastics. Whether on the floor, on the bars, on the beam, or in mid-air, each gymnastic movement demands certain shapes to be made. It is that skill of moving through one shape to another which makes gymnastics so exciting to watch. It is therefore important that you learn to use your whole body and understand the shape you are trying to make. Then, as your body becomes stronger and more supple, you will be able to improve the shapes that you achieve.

Kneeling on one leg
This shape can be used as a balance on the floor, or the beam. Make sure your raised leg is well stretched, and lift your head.

You can vary this shape by changing the position of your raised leg, or lifting one arm.

Dish
The dish is a basic shape, but it is important to learn because it is a strength move which will improve your posture, and help you in making many other moves.

Lie on your back and raise your arms, shoulders, and legs from the floor.

Press your lower back flat on the floor.

Arch
The arch is similar to the dish, but in reverse. Lie on your front and pull in your seat muscles as you lift your head, arms, upper body, and legs off the ground. Keep your head between your arms and make sure your legs are straight.

The bridge will require practice to perform really well as you will need to develop a supple back and shoulders.

Extend through your arms and legs.

Box splits
You will need lots of practice to make this shape. Start by sitting up straight with your legs stretched wide apart, in front of you. Aim to press your legs further back each time you try this.

Hold your arms out horizontally, or stretch them up above your head.

Do not let your knees roll inwards.

Your head should stay between your arms, so try not to let your chin strain upwards.

Improving suppleness
To condition your body and become a good gymnast will take years of practice. Your suppleness will improve with training, and you will be able to extend the range of shapes you can make and hold comfortably. Here, Hui Lan of China demonstrates the suppleness of her back and shoulders.

Be patient
Do not force your body into any positions that hurt or feel strained. Be patient – with practice your body will become more supple and you will be able to achieve most of the shapes shown here.

Back support
This is a strong position to hold. Your arms must be straight and directly under your shoulders. Pull in your stomach and seat muscles so that your body makes a straight line from your head to your feet.

Your fingers should point away from your toes.

Front support
Like the back support, this shape demands that the body is held in a straight line. Make sure that you keep your arms straight and that your hands are only shoulder-width apart.

Check that your hands are both in the same position.

Straighten your legs so that they slope from your hips to the floor in a straight line.

From this position you will eventually be able to kick your legs over, one at a time, to come back on to your feet in a move called a bridge kickover.

Keep your feet and legs together.

Bridge
To make a bridge, start by lying on your back with your knees bent up and your feet flat on the floor, close to your seat. Bend your elbows and place your hands on the floor either side of your head. Your fingers should point towards your feet and your elbows should point to the ceiling. Push up strongly from your hands and feet to raise your body into position, and straighten your legs.

Keep your feet flat on the floor.

Shapes in the air
Make sure you understand exactly what shape you are trying to show as you go through each stage of a movement. Here Annika Reeder of Great Britain shows a dramatic shape as she leaps high in the air.

Rolls and rolling

ROLLING IS is an important basic gymnastic skill that can be used in many different ways. In a roll, the weight of the body transfers from one body part to another, which makes rolling movements useful for linking a variety of shapes and skills together. On the floor, a roll itself can make an effective low shape. And because rolls can be made fast or slow, they can be used to change the pace of an exercise. If you watch gymnastics on television, you will see rolls being used creatively in all the gymnastic disciplines.

Log roll

The log roll is a useful move to turn smoothly from your front to your back, or from your back to your front. As you roll, your body weight must change from one body part to another in a controlled way, and each shape must be shown clearly.

Hold your arms shoulder-width apart.

Lift your legs and press them together.

1 Start in an arch shape and begin to roll on to your side. Be careful to maintain the tension in your body and keep your arms and legs fully extended.

2 On your side, your body should be in a straight line with your seat and stomach muscles pulled in, and your head between your arms. Continue rolling over.

3 From your side, roll on to your back and into a dish shape with your arms and legs lifted off the floor. Press your lower back flat to the floor.

2 As you roll, let your right elbow, right side, and then right shoulder touch the floor in turn. Roll up on to your right shoulder, lifting your seat off the floor. Then continue to roll across your back from your right shoulder to your left shoulder.

Do not let go of your legs, or let your elbows bend.

If you are very supple, you may be able to clasp your legs below your knees, or even at your ankles.

1 Start in a straddle sit. Place your hands on your knees, and lightly clasp your legs around the knee. Without changing the straddle sit shape, start to tip over towards your right side.

In the sitting position, keep your back straight and head up.

Circle roll

The circle, or teddy bear roll, is a fun roll that starts and finishes in the same position, but facing in a different direction. Interesting shapes and patterns can be made if you work with a partner or a group of four people.

Forward rolls

The shape of the forward roll is used in many gymnastic moves, so it is important to learn to roll correctly from the beginning. It is much harder to correct bad technique once it has become a habit.

Use your arms to help you balance.

Roll on the back of your head and neck.

Push off with your hands to bring yourself on to your feet.

1 Balance on the balls of your feet in a neat squat position.

2 Put your hands on the floor, tuck your head in and start to roll.

3 A strong push from your feet will roll your body over.

4 Reach out with your arms to help you come back into a squat position.

As you roll on to your shoulders, the weight of your legs in the air will help you to keep rolling.

Make sure your toes are pointed at all stages of the roll.

3 Continue rolling down your left side and elbow and on to the left side of your seat. Let the weight of your legs carry you over as you start sitting up from your left side.

4 Finally, roll across your seat, bringing your right leg down to the floor. You should finish the roll in the straddle position in which you started, but facing the opposite direction.

Starting and finishing positions

Forward rolls can start from, or finish in, a great variety of positions.

The roll may be taken from standing instead of squatting.

Practise coming back on to your feet and standing up at the end of the roll without using your hands to help you up.

A forward roll from a balance, such as an arabesque, is a useful linking move in a floor or beam exercise.

Roll on to the back of your head.

Pull up your supporting leg.

Relax your shoulders.

Do not let your hips twist.

A strong finishing position can make the roll an effective movement in a simple sequence.

Backward rolls

FROM THE SIMPLE shape of a backward roll, many other moves develop. The tightly tucked position of both backward and forward rolls is the basis of the tucked somersault. You will need to work on the move into, and out of, the tucked rolling position on the floor before you will be able to start learning a basic somersault, or go on to achieve a complicated vault. Backward rolls are a basic skill to master, but like other movements that travel backwards, you will probably find them harder to learn initially than movements that go forwards.

Rolling on a slope
Using a sloping surface can help you to learn a new skill. In the backward roll it helps you to turn over on to your feet. Working up a slope may also be used in training sessions to improve your strength and stamina.

Keep your knees and feet together and use your stomach muscles to pull up your legs.

Point your toes extending right through your feet and ankles.

Tuck your chin on to your chest.

A foam wedge or a springboard covered with a mat makes a good sloping surface to practise on.

How to do a backward roll
The backward roll needs to have enough speed and force to carry the movement through to the finish. Toppling backwards into the tight tuck position will make you start to roll, rounding your back will help to keep the motion going, and a strong push with your hands will carry the roll over to bring you back on to your feet.

Start with your head up and eyes looking straight ahead.

Use your arms to help you balance.

Your feet should be together and toes pointed.

2 Curl your back so that you roll along it from your seat to your shoulders. Bend your elbows and point them up to the ceiling as you put your hands on the floor either side of your head.

Keep your elbows high and close to your knees. Do not let them collapse on to the floor.

1 Start in a well-balanced squat position with your knees together and your back straight. To begin the movement, let you heels drop towards the floor so that you are off balance and you start to roll back on to your seat.

Keep your knees together.

Let your heels drop to start the rolling movement.

Start and finish positions

Like the forward roll, the backward roll can start from, or end in, many different positions, which is why it is such a useful linking movement. To finish kneeling on one knee, let one leg extend behind you as you come out of the roll. The straddle stand can be used to start or end the roll. You may find it fun to experiment with other start and finish positions.

Hold your head up.

Stretch your back leg out behind you.

Keep your back straight and parallel to the floor in this straddle stand position.

The slope helps you to lift your hips high and feel your weight moving on to your hands.

Learn to push up strongly through your hands and arms as your feet come down to the floor.

Keep your chin tucked in to keep your weight off the top of your head.

The finishing position can then be made on the floor.

Hand position

The push from your hands is the key stage of the roll. Make sure you position your hands correctly.

Put your palms flat on the floor, and point your fingers towards your shoulders.

Tucking up

Tuck your chin down on to your chest as you start to roll over in both backward and forward rolls.

Relax your shoulders. Try not to let them hunch up as you hold the finishing balance.

3 Push strongly from the floor and begin to straighten your arms. This will lift your hips high so that your body can roll over your head as your feet come down to the floor.

Your knees should not touch the floor.

4 The push off the floor, as you straighten your arms, should be strong enough to carry you through the final turning stage of the roll and back on to your feet.

Finish on your toes.

Balances

A BALANCE is a shape that a gymnast makes, and holds, poised on part of the body. Good posture is essential to balance work. To maintain a moment of stillness, the gymnast must be composed and have complete muscle control. A good balance will show stretch, poise, and a clear body line. So, whether you are holding a basic shape or a difficult balance, be aware of your whole body – from the expression on your face through to the extension in your fingertips and toes.

Beam balance
Shannon Miller shows a steady balance on one leg with the other leg raised in preparation for her next move. Each shape helps to make an effective beam exercise.

On one foot

1 One of the simplest balances on a small body part is on one foot. Stand with good posture and raise one leg in front of you by bending your knee.

Use your arms to help you balance.

2 Carry your raised leg round to the side, keeping the knee bent. Pull up through your supporting leg.

Do not let your hips twist.

3 Stretch and lift your free leg out to the side to hold a strong, balanced position.

Rising on to the ball of your foot, or lifting the free leg higher, will make this balance much more difficult.

V-sit balance

1 This seat balance starts easily but becomes more difficult as you lift your legs and arms. Start by sitting, with your hands and toes resting on the floor.

Look up at your toes.

2 Stretch your legs high in front of you and use your hands to steady yourself.

Do not let your back sag.

3 Finally, lift your arms up to complete the V-shape.

Only a small part of your seat remains on the floor.

Shoulder stand balance

Your body should stay flat on the floor until the final lift into the balance.

Press down with your fingers to steady yourself.

1 To start, lie on your back with the small of your back and the palms of your hands pressed into the floor.

2 Bend your legs up over your chest. Push down with your hands and start to lift your hips off the floor.

3 Stretch your legs up vertically and pull up through your body to hold the balance firmly.

Arabesques

An arabesque is an elegant balance on one leg with the other leg raised behind and the arms stretched out gracefully. In its many forms, it is widely used in girls' gymnastics. Arabesques can be performed with the front leg straight or bent, and the back leg can be kept low, or held high, but in all cases, your head and body should be poised to make an attractive line.

First arabesques
When you first start to practise arabesques, you will not be able to raise your leg very high. It is more important to concentrate on holding a good body shape.

Stepping into an arabesque
With practice you will be able to go into an arabesque from another movement.

Arabesque with supported leg
You will need to be supple and strong to hold an advanced arabesque position like this one.

Hold your leg around the knee.

Let your eyes follow the line of your arm.

Turn the palm of your hand down.

1 From a firm stance on one leg, clasp the knee of your raised leg with one hand. Keeping your knee bent, take your leg out to the side and then back behind you.

2 Keep holding your raised leg as you stretch it up behind you and lean forwards. As you do so, carry your opposite arm forwards.

This arm follows the line made by the raised leg.

Keep your back arched and your shoulders and head lifted.

Only take the leg as high as you comfortably can without twisting your hips, or losing your balance.

Try to link the stages into a continuous movement from start, to step, position, and hold.

Arm positions
Arm positions for an arabesque can be varied. Both arms can be held high or out to your sides, or with one arm carried forwards and one arm back. Whichever position you choose to take, the line of the arms should make the arabesque look balletic and graceful.

Bend your front knee.

Make sure your supporting foot does not roll inwards.

1 Stand in a poised start position with your arms up, your legs straight, and your feet together. Pull up through your body.

2 Take a lunge step, bending the knee of your front leg. Carry your arms down in a smooth and controlled movement.

3 Let your weight go forwards over your supporting leg and straighten that leg as you carry your back leg up behind you.

Headstands and handstands

BALANCING ON your head and hands is an important basic skill used in both boys' and girls' gymnastics. If you watch gymnastics, you will soon spot headstands and handstands being used in all sorts of ways, and with a great variety of leg positions. Because they are so widely used, you will probably start learning these skills early in your training. At first you will need help from your coach to reach and hold these balances. Then you will be ready to develop them by changing your leg positions, or by linking them with other moves.

Tucked headstand

The tucked headstand starts from a crouch. Position your head and hands on a mat and move your feet in to bring your hips over your head. With bent knees, lift up your feet. When you can balance like this, try straightening your legs into a stretched headstand.

Lift your hips high.

Keep your elbows bent.

Balance on your forehead, where your hairline begins, not on the top of your head.

On the bars
The handstand shape is required for swings and circles round the bars, shown here by Tatiana Gutsu of Ukraine.

Keep your head between your arms.

Hold a straight body line.

Stretch your arms up, keeping your shoulders down.

Stretch your back leg as you kick up.

Supported handstand

You will see the handstand shape used in floor, bar, beam, ring, and vault work. Before you can start to use it with other skills, you must learn to hold it as a perfect upright balance. Practise with support from your coach, or another gymnast, until you can perform a handstand and hold it, unaided, as a balance.

A partner can help by supporting you firmly at hip-level as you kick up into the handstand.

Give a good push off from your back foot to lunge forwards.

Bend your front knee into a lunge position.

1 At first you will start the handstand from a standing position. With your arms stretched above your head, take a long lunge step forwards and look to the point on the floor where you are going to place your hands.

2 As your hands go to the floor, kick up your back leg and push up from your front leg, straightening the knee. The upward swing of your back leg, combined with the pushing action from the front leg, will carry your front leg off the floor.

Push up strongly through your front leg and foot.

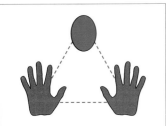

Head and hand position
Make a triangle with your forehead and hands on the mat. Place your hands shoulder-width apart and spread your fingers.

Equal weight
Spread your weight equally on your head and hands.

Straight leg headstand
Going into the stretched headstand with straight legs is a more advanced move. Start by kneeling, and position your head and hands on the mat.

Straighten your legs to push your hips up. Start to drag your feet towards your hands.

Keep your legs straight and lift them up until they are parallel to the floor.

Carry your legs up into the fully stretched headstand position.

Grip the floor with your fingers to hold yourself steady.

When you reach the handstand position, your partner can change grip to support you at the ankles.

3 As your second leg swings upright, press both legs together and stretch your feet and ankles. You should try to hold your body so that your ankles, knees, hips, shoulders, and hands are all in a straight line.

Your partner can help to correct your body position.

Giving support
Move in to support your partner as the legs swing up. Do not back away.

Pull in your stomach and seat muscles.

Do not let your back hollow or sag.

Look at your hands.

Place your hands on the floor, shoulder-width apart.

Spread your fingers and grip the floor to help steady the balance.

Cartwheels and round-offs

THE CARTWHEEL and the round-off start in a similar way. They are both turning moves performed on the hands with the legs swinging over the top. Both moves can be made on their own and this is how you will learn to do them. Usually, they are linked to other moves such as jumps or flips. You may have already attempted to do cartwheels for fun, but for the gymnast, cartwheels and round-offs are precise and useful skills. With practice you will be able to turn controlled cartwheels and use the speed and power of the round-off.

Cartwheels on the beam
On the beam, it is essential that cartwheels travel in a straight line, with very sure footwork. A cartwheeling action may be used to move out of a handstand balance.

How to do a cartwheel

A good cartwheel travels in a straight line. In time you will be able to try cartwheels putting one hand only on the floor, or even cartwheels with no hands. But first you will need to learn the basic cartwheel. Different start positions may be used. Here, the start is made facing the direction in which you will travel.

In a straight line
The pattern your hands and feet make should be hand, hand, foot, foot, in a straight line on the floor. Aim to travel a considerable distance as you wheel.

Keep your body straight so that your legs pass directly over your hands.

Lift your leg high and straight.

Stretch up through your body.

Reach forwards with your second arm so that it is well ahead of the first.

Step on to your raised leg.

Straighten this leg as your first hand goes to the floor.

1 Face the way you are going to move. Stand up straight and stretch your arms above your head. Lift one leg high and straight in front of you and step on to it.

Turn your hand outwards.

2 Lean to place one hand on the floor. Kick up your back leg to tip yourself on to your hands and straighten your supporting leg as you push off from it.

The round-off

The round-off, or arab spring, is a move that is used to build up speed in a sequence, leading into a jump or another agility. It starts like a cartwheel but includes a quarter turn, and your legs come together so that you land on two feet, facing the opposite way.

Stretch up and face forwards.

Hands down
Put your second hand down, out of line with your first hand.

Swing your legs up as if to cartwheel.

Your hands are already starting the turn.

Bring your legs together in the air.

Push off with your hands.

Swing your arms up to control your landing.

Land on two feet.

1 Face the way you are moving. Step forwards and spring on to your hands, one after the other.

2 As your first hand goes to the floor, kick up your back leg. Swing your other leg up and bring them together.

3 A strong push from your hands will help you to snap your legs down so that you land on two feet.

Split your legs wide apart in the side handstand position.

Keep your legs split wide apart.

Keep your knees straight and stretch your feet and ankles.

Hold your arms level and your shoulders down.

3 Place your other hand on the floor in line with the first. As your legs swing upwards you should turn sideways into a handstand position.

Your hands should be shoulder-width apart on the floor.

End your cartwheel standing sideways to the way you started, and with your feet apart.

Stretch your leading leg to the floor.

4 From the handstand position, carry on turning. Push off from your first hand and bring your leading leg down to the floor, in line with your hands.

5 A strong push-off with your hand, together with the movement of your legs coming down, one after the other, should bring you back to a standing position.

Push off the floor to wheel to your feet.

Finish in a stretched standing position.

Backflips and walkovers

A S YOU MAKE progress with your training, you will start to learn some more advanced moves. All the work you have done so far will help you now. At first the idea of falling back and going over on to your hands may seem frightening. Backward movements such as the walkover and backflip are difficult to learn, but they are essential moves if you are to continue improving your gymnastic skills. With help from your coach to learn all the preparatory stages, you will find them exciting skills to master.

Back walkover

The back walkover is normally used in conjunction with other moves, and can be performed quickly or slowly.

Reach for the floor.

Extend your leading leg.

Push off from this foot.

1 Start with your leading leg raised and move your arms backwards, letting your head drop between them, and arching your back.

2 Lift your leading leg high and as your hands reach the floor, push up through your supporting leg.

How to do a backflip

Never try this without your coach. All gymnasts aim to do a backflip, but it is an advanced move and there are many preparatory skills to learn first. The backflip is often used to build up speed for another move, such as a somersault.

Swing your arms up over your head.

Straighten your legs.

Bend your knees.

Preparatory skills
Do not attempt the backflip until you have mastered all the preparatory skills and your coach is there to help you.

Push off the floor through your legs and feet.

First backflips
At first, you will be taught to backflip from a standing position to finish standing on two feet. Then you may learn to do it from a back walkover or a round-off.

Start to look for your landing spot on the floor.

Point your toes and extend through your ankles.

1 Start in a standing position, with your feet together, and bend your knees. Lean back in an off-balance position, taking your arms back behind you.

2 Spring off the floor with a strong push from your feet and legs, and swing your arms upwards over your head. Straighten your legs and let your hips lift up.

3 Let your legs drive your body upwards and backwards, but make sure you keep your head back between your arms as you start to reach for the floor.

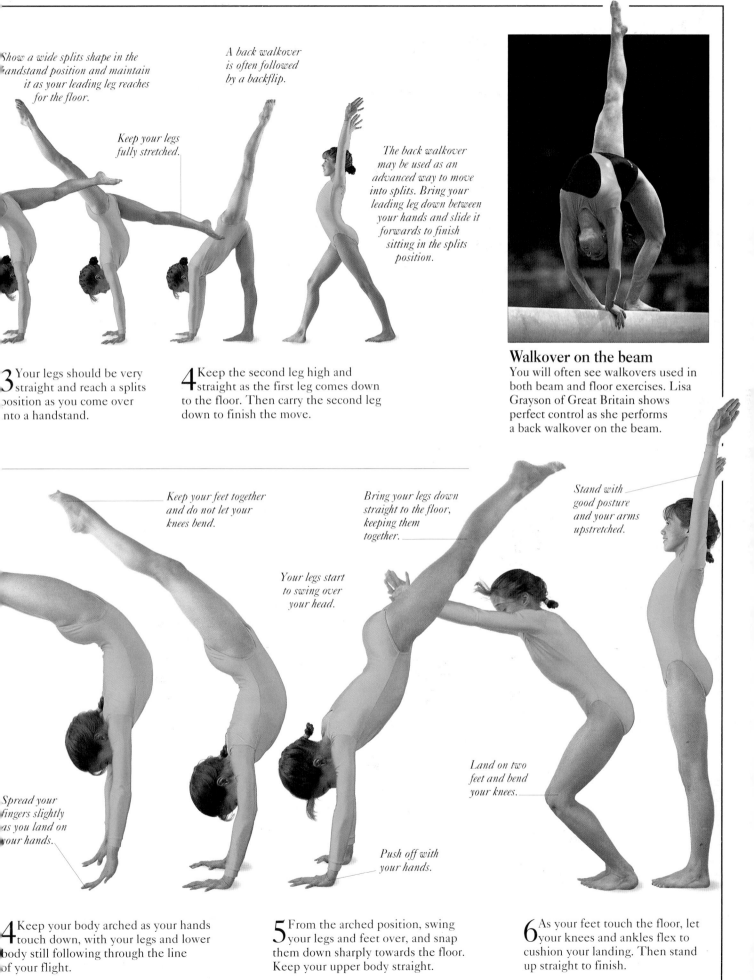

Show a wide splits shape in the handstand position and maintain it as your leading leg reaches for the floor.

Keep your legs fully stretched.

A back walkover is often followed by a backflip.

The back walkover may be used as an advanced way to move into splits. Bring your leading leg down between your hands and slide it forwards to finish sitting in the splits position.

3 Your legs should be very straight and reach a splits position as you come over into a handstand.

4 Keep the second leg high and straight as the first leg comes down to the floor. Then carry the second leg down to finish the move.

Walkover on the beam

You will often see walkovers used in both beam and floor exercises. Lisa Grayson of Great Britain shows perfect control as she performs a back walkover on the beam.

Keep your feet together and do not let your knees bend.

Bring your legs down straight to the floor, keeping them together.

Stand with good posture and your arms upstretched.

Your legs start to swing over your head.

Spread your fingers slightly as you land on your hands.

Land on two feet and bend your knees.

Push off with your hands.

4 Keep your body arched as your hands touch down, with your legs and lower body still following through the line of your flight.

5 From the arched position, swing your legs and feet over, and snap them down sharply towards the floor. Keep your upper body straight.

6 As your feet touch the floor, let your knees and ankles flex to cushion your landing. Then stand up straight to finish.

Jumps and leaps

JUMPING AND leaping movements are used by all gymnasts. A jump usually takes off from two feet and lands on two feet. In a leap, the take-off is from one foot, with the landing on the other foot. Together, you can use jumps and leaps to link acrobatic skills or as part of your dance movements in your floor and beam sequences. Good vaulting and mounts on to the beam or bars also demand strong jumping actions. Experiment, and you will find that you can make lots of different shapes in the air by varying your leg and arm positions as you jump and leap.

Stag leap

The stag leap is a popular and attractive move that you will often see in floor and beam work. It takes its name from the shape the back leg makes as it bends and lifts. You can vary the leap by straightening your front leg in the air, or by taking both your arms upwards.

Point your toes.

Lift your back leg as high as you can.

Keep your back straight.

Swing your arms upwards.

Try to get good height from the push-off.

Swing your front leg high.

1 You can practise this move as a standing jump from two feet. Later you can use one or two steps to turn it into a leap travelling forwards. Start with good posture and take one step. The leg that you step on to will be the leg that you kick up behind you.

2 As you step, swing your other leg forwards into a high leap. Push off from your stepping foot and swing your arms up to gain as much height as possible as you travel forwards and upwards.

Step forwards, ready to leap.

Push off from this foot.

Turn your head slightly over your front shoulder.

Raise your arms to shoulder-height.

*old your
ad up
nd relax
ur
oulders.*

Do not let your hips twist.

Your front leg lifts then descends to a soft landing.

3 Lift your back leg high and bend it up behind ou to make the stag shape. end your front knee and ake one arm forwards and he other one back.

Land softly on your front foot.

Stretch your feet and ankles.

plit leap
ina Gogean of Romania ows a split leap on the eam. A strong upswing of er arms has helped her to chieve great height in the eap, and by keeping her rms up, she makes a stong ape which adds to the eling of height.

Shapes to make

You can make hundreds of different shapes in the air when you jump. The higher you jump, the more time you will have to make the shape. Always flex your knees as you land, and try to land softly.

Make sure your back stays straight.

Straddle pike jump
In the air, straddle your legs and stretch them out. At the same time, bend forwards from your hips to make the pike position.

Extend through your feet and ankles.

Tuck jump
Bend your knees up tightly in front of your body as you jump. Use the swing of your arms upwards to help you travel up and not along.

Keep your head lifted.

Bring your knees up to your chest.

Star jump
Try to make a symmetrical shape in the star jump. Your arms should stretch out at the same angle as each other, and so should your legs.

Stretch out through your arms, body, and legs.

Show a wide straddle position with your legs.

Making a sequence

ONCE YOU have learned a few skills, you can start linking them together to make a sequence. In a major competition, artistic gymnasts perform two exercises on each piece of apparatus. First they all have to perform the same sequence as each other in the compulsory, or set, exercise. Then, in the voluntary exercise they can include some of their favourite skills. When you make up a sequence, include the things you can do well, and then try to put in some changes of speed and height to make your work really interesting to watch.

Kick your leading leg up, as you go into the round-off.

Stretch up through your body.

Start this sequence ready to move into a round-off.

Begin the turning movement on your han...

A girl's floor exercise

Girls perform floor exercises to music and an exercise lasts between 70 and 90 seconds. Pa... of the skill of a good performance is to interp... the mood of the music by the dance steps, ju... leaps, balances, and turns you use, and the w... you link the steps together. The sequence shown here includes a series of agilities and includes two changes of direction.

Shapes and joins
Try to show clear shapes at every stage of your sequence, and join each move smoothly.

A boy's floor exercise

A boy's floor exercise should be designed to show the gymnast's strength and control. You will see that many of the same skills are used in both boys' and girls' sequences but boys do not perform to music. So, although the boys' exercises must be artistic, they use jumps and strength elements, rather than dance elements.

Hold the inside of your heel.

Make your dive as high and long as you can.

Keep your legs together and straight.

Take your arms back, ready to swing forwards.

3 Swing your arms forwards to give you lift, and let your legs drive you upwards and forwards into a dive forward roll.

Look ahead your landi... poin...

In competition, a held balance must be included in the boys' floor exercise.

Reach for the floor.

1 This sequence starts with a Y-balance. Hold your balance for two seconds.

2 Bring your free leg down and turn as you step forwards on to it. Spring from two feet into a dive.

Dive roll
You must only attempt the dive roll on a gymnastics floor, or with good mats to land on.

Swing your second leg up and snap both legs down together to land.

Bring your legs together.

From the acceleration of the round-off, spring into a backflip.

Look for the floor.

Start to split your legs ready to land on one foot.

Bring one leg over first.

As your hands reach the floor, swing your legs over, showing the split position clearly.

Point your toes.

Finish with a smile even if you made a mistake.

From the roll, come straight to standing and finish with poise and good posture.

With your chin on your chest, tuck into a forward roll.

From your handstand, tip into a forward roll.

Kick into a handstand balance.

Land your backflip on one foot, bringing your second leg down behind.

Push with your hands.

Keep your arms straight.

Land on this foot.

6 Then kick up to a steady handstand.

Point your toes.

7 Move your hands in quarter-turns to turn your body.

8 Finish your handstand pirouette facing the opposite way.

4 Land on your hands, tuck your head in, and roll on the back of your neck.

5 Roll on to your feet and come up to stand.

Tuck down into the roll.

Press your legs together.

Stretch your arms up to help you come up to a standing position.

Keep your body straight.

Do not let your back hollow.

Take your weight on your hands.

Roll on the back of your neck and shoulders.

Spread your fingers and grip the floor.

Walk round on your hands.

Vaulting

VAULTING IS one of the most exciting events in gymnastics, and top gymnasts now perform vaults of amazing difficulty. They often include somersaults and turns, and even take-offs with a turn so that the vault is performed backwards. When you start to vault, you will have to practise all the preparatory stages, beginning with exercises using the springboard, learning to land safely, and jumping on to and off the vaulting horse.

Down to earth
For safety, always land on two feet when you jump from a height or vault.

Swing your arms up straight.

Keep your feet together and your legs and body straight.

3 Place your hands squarely on top of the horse. Make sure that you hold a straight handstand shape all the way over.

Handspring vault

A handspring is a simple vault. In this sequence you can see the stages of the vault: the take-off, the flight on to the horse, the handspring itself, the flight off the horse, and the landing. When you start to practise vaulting, you will discover that every vault can be divided into these stages.

1 Start with a strong, fast, even run-up to the springboard. From the run, make a hurdle step so that your feet land together on the springiest part of the board.

2 Swing your arms forwards and upwards as you make the jump from the springboard. Keep your body straight in the flight on to the horse.

Your head should stay between your arms.

Take off with a high, upward jump from two feet.

At take-off, your feet should be slightly in front of your body.

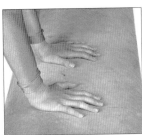

Hands on
Your hands should be shoulder-width apart as they make contact with the horse. Spread your fingers slightly to take your weight.

Vaulting horse

The springiest part of the board is about 20 cm from the raised end.

The horse can be made lower for junior gymnasts.

Women's vault

Women always vault across the width of the horse. They can vault twice in competition but only the higher of the two marks counts. Here, Svetlana Boguinskaya of Belarus performs a Yurchenko full twist – named, like many gymnastic moves, after the gymnast who first performed it internationally. From this height she will complete the twist and straighten out to land.

Men's vault

Men always vault along the length of the horse. In competition, the men get only one attempt at their chosen vault. Here, Valeri Liukin of Ukraine shows a Kasamatsu vault. One hand follows the other on to the horse, and the vault finishes with a turn.

Your hands come off the horse as soon as your legs start to come over.

With good body tension, you may show a dish shape.

Keep your arms stretched above your head.

5 Straighten your body as you come down to land. Land on the balls of your feet, quickly lowering your heels to the floor, and flexing your knees and ankles.

Straighten your body.

4 As you come over the horse, push off, extending through your whole body to start your flight off the horse.

Aim to get a good distance between the horse and your landing point.

You will lose points for an unsteady landing.

Hands off

Try to push off to get height in your flight off the horse. Aim to show space between your hands and the top of the horse.

Vaulting in competition

In a major competition, the value of each type of vault depends on how difficult it is to perform. A difficult vault with turns or somersaults will be marked out of 10.00 points. A handspring is considered to be a simple vault and is marked out of only 8.50 points. Even if you perform it perfectly, you cannot score more than 8.50 points.

Flex your knees and ankles.

Land with your feet together.

The balance beam

THE BEAM, or balance beam, is used only in girls' gymnastics. In competition, gymnasts have to perform a sequence of balances, jumps, agilities, and turns. Each move should flow freely into the next, with the gymnasts only pausing to hold the balance positions. Some of the skills may be simple to perform at floor-level, but they become much more difficult when executed on the beam, and many gymnasts fear it. You will need to spend long hours perfecting your technique on the floor to build up enough confidence to move freely on this apparatus.

The mount can be made to the side or end of the beam.

Mounts and dismounts

There are many ways to get on and off the beam to start and finish an exercise. A springboard may be used to mount the beam and, in competition, bonus marks may be awarded for a difficult mount, such as a front somersault. But points will be lost for a fall, so it is better to be safe than sorry.

On the beam

When you have practised and mastered skills on the floor, the next step will be to work on a low beam or bench until you are controlled and very confident. Then you will be able to move on to a practice beam surrounded by safety mats, which can be built up to the height of the beam, and gradually removed as you make progress.

Lift your leg high and complete the Y shape with your free arm.

Keep your arms level with each other.

Hold the balance still for two seconds.

Do not let your body twist.

Before trying any advanced balances and jumps, you will learn to walk, turn, and sit on the beam.

Extend your foot.

Hold your head up and shoulders down.

Grip the sides of the beam with your fingers.

V-sit

A beam exercise must include moves low on the beam, such as this V-sit. From this position the gymnast could push up into a bridge shape or lie back into a backward roll.

Y-balance

The elegant Y-balance is a difficult shape to hold, but attractive balances are an important part of a beam exercise. Keeping your head up, and fixing your eyes on a point in the distance, will help you to hold a balance.

The difficulty of a balance can be increased by performing it up on your toes.

Beam practice

A coloured foam strip is sometimes used to mark the width and length of the beam so that gymnasts can practise moves for the beam, or work out a sequence, safely at floor-level.

Jump with confidence and try to land lightly.

A cabriole jump

Neat footwork is very important on the beam and work should be performed on your toes.

In competition

Shannon Miller holds a handstand balance on the beam. In competition, points are awarded for the difficulty of the moves shown, but it is wise not to include moves you cannot do well. Points are deducted for lack of technique, and you will lose 0.5 of a point for a fall.

W-jump

It is important to show a variety of jumps and leaps during the exercise. The elegant W-jump is a favourite with gymnasts on the beam.

Keep your head up and your eyes fixed on a point in the distance.

Jump sequences

Major competitions require a sequence of two or more jumps. Practise linking different jumps, one after the other, with no step in between.

Try to get as much height as possible when you jump.

2 The shape that you make in the air defines the sort of jump you are making. In the W-jump, one leg stretches forwards horizontally, with the heel of the other foot tucked up beneath you.

3 Let your knees flex to help you land softly, but steadily. Use your arms to help you maintain your balance.

Steady landings

In a competition, the judges will look for steady landings. Points will be deducted if you wobble or lose your balance.

1 Try to show good posture, with your head up and back straight at all stages of the jump. Start in a poised position, and with one step, take off from both feet.

Flex your knees as you land, ready to jump again, or go into your next move.

Rhythmic gymnastics

R HYTHMIC GYMNASTICS is a branch of
gymnastics for girls. If you like the balletic
side of gymnastics and working to music, you will
enjoy learning rhythmic skills. Rhythmic work takes
place on a carpeted floor area 12 metres square. The
gymnasts perform dance movements to music while
using hand apparatus. At first, you will spend a lot of
time learning to use the apparatus. In time you will
be able to throw, catch, and use it to make
interesting shapes, and to link it with
dance, leaps, balances, turns,
and a variety of low and
high moves.

*The swivel helps to
stop the ribbon
tangling.*

Silk ribbon

*Keep your
eyes on the
ribbon.*

*Keep the ribbon
moving all the
time.*

*Raise your
arm above
your head.*

Working with the ribbon

Ribbon work is very attractive to watch as the
ribbon circles and spirals around the gymnast.
Use a large arm movement to keep the ribbon
moving along its entire length. The ribbon
should not touch any part of your body, nor
become entangled in any way.

*Stretch up into an
elegant arabesque
balance.*

*The ribbon is 7 m
long and attached
to a wand.*

Swivel

Apparatus

There are five pieces of apparatus
and in time, you will learn how
to handle each of them. Many
gymnasts find the clubs difficult
to use and you will probably
learn to use them last.

*Balls should be 18-
20 cm in diameter
and weigh 400 g.*

Wand

Hoop

*Hoops are usually made of plastic.
They should be between 80 cm
and 90 cm in diameter.*

*Wooden or plastic
clubs*

Rope

*The rope may be knotted
at the ends but must have no
handles. Its length depends
on the height of the gymnast.*

Group work

As a rhythmic gymnast, you may perform on
your own or work in a group of six. In group
work you can use different pieces of apparatus –
here a Bulgarian team is using hoops and
balls. The team is shown in its finishing
position at the end of the group sequence.

Hoop sequence

You can use hoops in many ways to create an effective sequence. You can swing them around your body, roll them on the floor, throw them in the air, or jump through them.

Carry your free arm up as you jump.

Turn your head slightly.

Look at your free hand.

Swing the hoop around your waist.

Balance on one leg.

Catch the hoop with both hands, then let one side drop.

Stay up on your toes.

Jump through the hoop.

Carry the hoop out to the side to finish.

Rope work

Ropes can be used for skipping steps. They can also be thrown, folded, or wrapped around you. The simple moves shown here will give you some ideas to practise.

Hold your arms well out from your body.

Watch the rope.

The loop of rope will fall back.

Now you have folded the rope into four, ready to use in different ways.

As the rope swings up, stop it by lifting up your hands.

Stretch out your hands and catch the rope in the middle.

Skip on one foot as you turn the rope backwards.

Point your toes as you skip.

Stay up on your toes. This foot position is called demi-pointe.

Balance on one leg and twirl the ends of the rope.

Ball balance

This move with the ball is called a spiral. Here it is taken from kneeling and rises to finish in an arabesque. The ball must stay balanced on the palm of your hand. It must not touch your wrist, nor be grasped.

Lift the ball high.

Look up at the ball.

Pull up through your body.

Keep your arm straight and circle the ball behind you.

Kneel on one leg, rest one hand on the floor, and start with the ball held low in front of you.

Straighten your arm.

Carry the ball out to the side.

Bring the ball round to your other side.

Hold a graceful arm position.

Rise into an arabesque balance.

Bend your body in a full side bend.

Rise on demi-pointe.

Sports acrobatics

SPORTS acrobatics is a gymnastic sport that developed from acrobatic circus performers and balancing acts seen in displays and shows. Today, the sport has two branches: balance work and tumbling. For balance work, you will need to master gymnastic skills, such as jumps, leaps, turns, and acrobatic moves. You will also learn to work with a partner, or in a group, to achieve spectacular balance positions. Sports acrobatic routines are performed to music on a sprung floor 12 metres square. They include both the balance elements and individual skills.

Keep your body upright and very still.

You can use a variety of arm positions. Hold your arms out sideways, upwards, or take one arm forwards.

Into position
Move slowly and steadily into each balance position. When you are perfectly steady, hold the balance for at least two seconds.

Hold your body in a straight line.

Keep your arms straight to support yourself.

Stretch your back leg.

Spread your feet slightly apart.

Straighten your legs.

Support your partner under one knee, and the thigh of her extended leg.

Base and top
In pairs' work, the gymnast on the floor is called the base. The supported partner is called the top. In this simple balance, the base supports the weight of the top on his knees and arms.

Entries and exits
You can make your work interesting and attractive to watch by using imaginative ways to get into, and out of, the balance positions.

Take your partner's weight equally on both your legs.

Press your back and arms into the floor to steady the balance.

Groups of four
Boys and men may compete in groups of four. In this Bulgarian group, the mid-position is balanced only on his arms, while the top holds a one-armed balance.

Stag balance
The stag balance shows the essence of mixed pairs' work. The elegance and grace of the top contrasts with the strength and steadiness of the base. To reach this position, the base bends his legs. Once the top is in place, the base straightens his legs to lift the balance.

Balances must be held for two seconds.

Boys may perform as a pair or as a group of four.

Counterbalance

A counterbalance is when you use your weight against your partner's weight. Both of you must keep good body tension as you lean away from each other. When you first try this balance, ask another person to help the top into position.

Look at your partner.

Stretch out your free arm in line with your body.

Don't let your head drop back.

Clasp hands firmly.

Maintain good body tension.

A Ukrainian boys' pair shows a difficult one-armed balance.

Lean back.

Point your toes.

Bend your knees.

You can vary this balance by using different leg positions.

A firm hold

It is essential that you both take a firm hold. Grip hands and clasp your fingers.

Three exercises

In competition, the teams perform three exercises. The first is called balance and includes a set number of balances. The next exercise is called tempo, in which the base throws and catches the top. The third exercise includes both balance and tempo moves.

Spread your feet apart.

Keep your back straight.

Hand position

Cup your partner's shoulders in the heels of your hands.

Straight arms

Shoulder balance

The shoulder balance is simple and stable. The base has a large part of his body on the floor and the top has several points of support. From here, the top may move her hands to her partner's hands or arms and extend to an advanced balance only on the arms.

Lift up your head.

Stretch and lift your legs.

Your arms, and those of your partner, should be straight and shoulder-width apart.

Press your back flat to the floor.

Palm to palm

Support with palm to palm contact and use your fingers to add control.

Stand with your feet apart to give yourself a wide base.

Straddle lever balance

This is an advanced balance that requires great strength from the base. The top rises into a lever position with her legs widely straddled and lifted.

Girls' trio

Girls can compete in a group of three. Here a Latvian trio shows a complicated balance. Each gymnast is using her weight to counterbalance the others, while forming an exciting shape.

Tumbling

TUMBLING IS another branch of sports acrobatics and, like the balance work, boys and girls both take part. The gymnasts, or tumblers, work on a sprung strip of floor 25 metres long and 1.5 metres wide. On this surface they perform an exercise called a tumble run. The tumblers travel in a straight line and accelerate as they perform a series of fast agilities, joining them one after the other, without pausing. To become a tumbler, you will have to start by mastering basic gymnastic skills. Then, as you make progress, you will work on round-offs, backflips, and somersaults and learn to link them with other agilities.

Starting a tumble run
A springboard may be used at the start of the run. It will help you to add height and speed to your opening move.

Tumble runs

Here you can see two different tumble runs. In competition, each tumbler performs three separate runs and must include different elements in each of them.

1 This run starts with a handspring.

Step on to your raised leg.

Swing your back leg up.

Spring on to both hands.

2 Push off strongly with your hands to lift yourself from the floor.

Bring your legs together.

Land on one foot.

3 Step straight into a round-off on your free leg.

Stretch out your free leg.

Scoring in competition
The scores from the tumbler's three runs are added together to make a possible total of 30 points. All the runs must go in one direction from start to finish. If the tumbler falls, or adds an extra step, the run is judged to be finished and no further part of it will be marked.

Safety mats
When you learn acrobatic skills, use plenty of safety mats to cushion any bad landings.

Stretch your lower legs and feet.

2 From the take-off, tuck into a somersault. Keep your elbows close to your body.

Jump upwards using your arms to help the movement.

1 Here, the tumble run opens with a forward somersault from a fast run-up.

Open out to land on one foot.

Stretch out your free leg and lunge on to it.

If you land on one foot, you must step into the next move with your free leg. Do not put in any extra steps, or pauses.

Kick your back leg up.

3 Move straight into a round-off with a lunge step forwards.

Reach for the floor.

Keep your head between your arms.

The round-off will turn you ready to make the next move backwards.

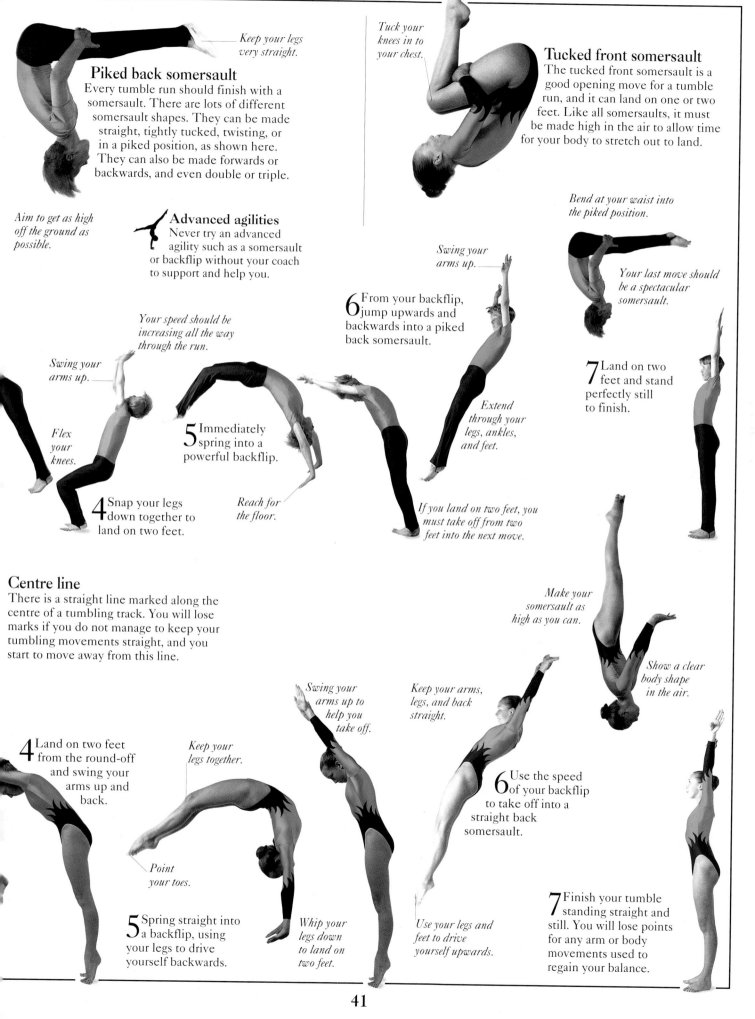

Piked back somersault
Every tumble run should finish with a somersault. There are lots of different somersault shapes. They can be made straight, tightly tucked, twisting, or in a piked position, as shown here. They can also be made forwards or backwards, and even double or triple.

Keep your legs very straight.

Aim to get as high off the ground as possible.

Advanced agilities
Never try an advanced agility such as a somersault or backflip without your coach to support and help you.

Tuck your knees in to your chest.

Tucked front somersault
The tucked front somersault is a good opening move for a tumble run, and it can land on one or two feet. Like all somersaults, it must be made high in the air to allow time for your body to stretch out to land.

Bend at your waist into the piked position.

Your last move should be a spectacular somersault.

Your speed should be increasing all the way through the run.

Swing your arms up.

6 From your backflip, jump upwards and backwards into a piked back somersault.

Swing your arms up.

Flex your knees.

5 Immediately spring into a powerful backflip.

Reach for the floor.

Extend through your legs, ankles, and feet.

7 Land on two feet and stand perfectly still to finish.

4 Snap your legs down together to land on two feet.

If you land on two feet, you must take off from two feet into the next move.

Centre line
There is a straight line marked along the centre of a tumbling track. You will lose marks if you do not manage to keep your tumbling movements straight, and you start to move away from this line.

Make your somersault as high as you can.

Show a clear body shape in the air.

4 Land on two feet from the round-off and swing your arms up and back.

Keep your legs together.

Swing your arms up to help you take off.

Keep your arms, legs, and back straight.

6 Use the speed of your backflip to take off into a straight back somersault.

Point your toes.

5 Spring straight into a backflip, using your legs to drive yourself backwards.

Whip your legs down to land on two feet.

Use your legs and feet to drive yourself upwards.

7 Finish your tumble standing straight and still. You will lose points for any arm or body movements used to regain your balance.

Competitions

GYMNASTICS lends itself to competition because it is a beautiful and dynamic sport to watch. Competitions can be arranged to suit different age groups and all levels of ability. If you would like to compete, there are many opportunities for you to do so in all branches of gymnastics. At the lowest level you can work to pass basic gymnastics awards. Then, you may find it fun to take part in matches arranged between your school or club and other clubs. In this way you will gradually progress and compete against more experienced gymnasts. At the highest level, there are national and international competitions. Very few gymnasts reach this level, but if you know a little bit about the major events you will find them all the more exciting to watch.

Dance, drama, and dynamics
Shannon Miller uses her talent for dance, dramatic touches, and dynamic agilities to excel in the floor exercise.

Rules and regulations
For every country, the *Fédération Internationale de Gymnastique* (FIG) is the overall governing body of artistic and rhythmic gymnastics. The FIG produces a Code of Points which is the rule book for all the high-level artistic and rhythmic events, such as the Olympic Games and World Championships. Sports acrobatics is not yet an Olympic sport. It has its own governing body, the International Federation of Sports Acrobatics (IFSA), which sets the rules for that sport.

Competition programme
Throughout the year, each country holds its own competitions. From these, the best gymnasts are selected to be in the national senior or junior teams. Each country also has a programme of international competitions which take place both at home and abroad. Even at international level, some events are arranged for different age groups. There are competitions for a senior team, an under-15 team, and even an under-12 team.

Major international competitions

Olympic Games
These are held once every 4 years and include artistic and rhythmic gymnastics.

Artistic World Championships
These are held every year but the events included, e.g. team or individual events, are varied in alternate years.

Rhythmic World Championships
This event is held every year.

Sports Acrobatics World Championships
This event is held every year.

Junior World Championships
Separate championships for each of the gymnastic disciplines are held every 2 years.

World Student Games
This competition is held every 2 years and includes artistic and rhythmic gymnastics.

World School Games
This event is held every two years and includes artistic and rhythmic gymnastics.

Judges and judging
In a major artistic competition there are six judges and a technical advisor to watch each exercise. Moves in the exercise are given a value, depending on how difficult they are to perform.

Judges use symbols like these as a quick way to note the moves they see in an exercise.

Double turn   Handspring   Arabesque

The technical advisor adds up the value of all the moves, the content, and the possible bonus points and tells the judges the maximum score that they can give if the exercise has been performed perfectly. From this score, the judges deduct points for any mistakes they have spotted during the exercise.

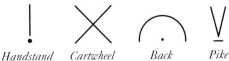

Handstand   Cartwheel   Back walkover   Pike jump

Rhythmic
In a major rhythmic competition, there are two panels of six judges. Six judges mark the technical content of the exercise while the other six judge the performance.

At the 1993 World Championships in Birmingham, Great Britain

Medal winners
Shannon Miller on the podium with silver medallist, Gina Gogean of Romania and bronze medallist, Tatiana Lisenko of Ukraine.

Sports acrobatics
In tumbling and balance work, competitors perform three exercises to score a possible total of 30 points. There are six judges, but the highest and lowest scores are left out. The score awarded for each exercise is the average of the other four scores.

Glossary

During your gymnastics classes, or when watching gymnastics, you may find it helpful to understand some of the following words and phrases.

A

Agility A gymnastic move of an acrobatic nature, such as a cartwheel, as opposed to dance movements or jumps.

Apparatus The equipment on which gymnasts work, or rhythmic gymnasts use.

Artistic gymnastics A competitive sport for girls and boys in which they perform exercises on gymnastics apparatus.

Asymmetrical When two parts of a whole are not the same. The two bars of the asymmetric bars are at different heights, for example.

B

Balance exercise A sports acrobatics exercise that involves held balances.

Base The name for the gymnast who supports the weight of the other or others in sports acrobatics.

Body tension Contraction of the muscles with no visible change in body shape.

Bonus points Extra points awarded by judges for some very difficult moves, or combinations of moves.

C

Chalk Magnesium carbonate, which some gymnasts dust on to their hands and feet to prevent slipping.

Code of Points The rule book issued by the FIG for coaches, judges, and gymnasts, from which competition rules are written.

Compulsory exercises Also known as set exercises. Exercises set by the governing body, which must be performed exactly as written down and illustrated.

D

Demi-pointe A term used in rhythmic gymnastics to mean "on your toes".

Discipline Rhythmic and artistic gymnastics, and sports acrobatics are all gymnastic sports, or disciplines.

Dismount The move you use to get off the apparatus.

E

Element A gymnastic move, or one essential part of an exercise.

Execution How well or skillfully a move or exercise is performed.

Extend To stretch to the maximum.

F

FIG The *Fédération Internationale de Gymnastique* is the governing body of world artistic and rhythmic gymnastics.

Flex To bend in a controlled manner.

Flexibility The ability to bend freely, without strain.

Flight Movement through the air either on to, or from, apparatus, or in acrobatic moves.

H

Handguards Leather guards to protect your hands when you work on the bars.

Held balance A poised position that you hold still for a moment.

Hurdle step A step from one foot landing on two feet in order to take off from both feet when using a springboard.

I

IFSA The International Federation of Sports Acrobatics is the governing body for that gymnastics discipline.

L

Line The shape made by positioning your body and limbs.

Lunge A position with one foot well in front of the other, with the front knee bent and most of your weight over it.

M

Mount The way you get on to the apparatus. It may be a difficult and daring move to score bonus points.

P

Pike A position in which your body and legs form a V-shape as you raise your legs high and straight, together or straddled.

Pirouette A spin or turn, which may be made on your hands or feet.

Posture The carriage of your body, or the way in which you hold yourself.

R

Rebound To bounce from something, such as a springboard.

Release and catch A term used to describe letting go of the bar, performing a move in mid-air, and catching the bar again.

Rhythmic gymnastics A form of gymnastics for girls only, using small pieces of hand-held apparatus and combining dance and gymnastic moves.

Routine A full exercise consisting of all the moves performed by a gymnast.

S

Score box An electronic device into which the judges enter scores to relay them to a central computer.

Sequence A series of gymnastic moves linked together by dance and jumps.

Somersault A full rotation of the body, performed in the air.

Sports acrobatics A form of gymnastics for boys and girls that includes balance work in pairs, trios, and fours, and tumbling work.

Stamina Your endurance, or ability to perform exercises many times without tiring.

Straddle A position with your legs stretched wide apart.

Suppleness The ability to bend all parts of the body well, and with stretchable muscles.

Symmetrical When the two sides, or parts, of a whole look identical. A star jump forms a symmetrical shape.

T

Technical advisor Also known as the technical expert or scientific technical collaborator. An official who advises the judges of the maximum possible score for an exercise, according to the Code of Points.

Technique The method or way in which you perform a gymnastic skill.

Tempo exercise The sports acrobatics exercise in which one gymnast is thrown or boosted into the air by another.

Top The name for the gymnast in sports acrobatics who is supported by the base.

Tuck A position in which you bring your knees up to your chest.

Tumbling A series of gymnastic agilities joined into a continuous run, without pauses or extra steps between the moves.

V

Voluntary exercises The exercises that a gymnast chooses to perform in competition.

W

Warm-up The essential preparation at the start of every training session to prevent injury. Warm-up exercises make your heart beat faster, increase breathing rate, and loosen joints and muscles, ready for work.

Index

A

acrobats 9
agilities 24, 25, 26, 30, 34, 40, 41, 42, 43
arabesque 17, 21, 36, 37, 42
arab spring *see* round-off
arch 14, 16
artistic apparatus 10, 11, 12, 13, 32, 34
artistic gymnastics 9, 12, 13, 42, 43
asymmetric bars 9, 12, 13, 43
awards 10, 42

B

backflip 26, 27, 31, 40, 41
back support 15
backward roll 18, 19, 34
balance 9, 14, 17, 20, 21, 22, 30, 34, 36, 37, 38, 39
balance beam 9, 12, 13, 14, 17, 20, 22, 27, 28, 34, 35
balance exercise 39, 43
ball 9, 36, 37
bars 11, 13, 14, 20, 22, 28
base 38, 39, 43
Boguinskaya, Svetlana 33
box splits 14
bridge 14, 15, 34
bridge kickover 15

C

cabriole jump 35
cartwheel 24, 25, 42, 43
chalk 11, 43
chalk buckets 12
circle roll 16
clothes 10
club 10, 11, 42
clubs (apparatus) 9, 36
coach 10, 11, 13, 22, 26, 41
Code of Points 42, 43
competition arena 13
competitions 8, 10, 11, 12, 13, 30, 33, 35, 38, 39, 40, 42
compulsory exercise 30, 43
counterbalance 39

D

demi-pointe 37, 43
Di, Fan 13
Diamidov turn 12
disciplines 9, 16, 43
dish 14, 16, 33
dismount 34, 43
dive forward roll 30
dumbbells 9

E

entries 38
exits 38

F

FIG 42, 43, 45
floor 9, 11, 13, 14, 16, 20, 22, 34, 35, 38
floor exercise 13, 17, 27, 30, 31
forward roll 17, 18, 19, 30, 31
front support 15

G

Gogean, Gina 29, 42
Grayson, Lisa 27
gymnasium 9, 10, 11, 12

H

hair 11
handguards 10, 11, 43
handspring 40, 42
handspring vault 32, 33
handstand 13, 22, 23, 24, 25, 27, 31, 32, 35, 42
handstand pirouette 31
headstand 22, 23
hoop 9, 36, 37
horizontal bar 9, 13
hurdle step 32, 43

I

IFSA 42, 43, 45

J

Jahn, F. 9
jewellery 10
judges 13, 42
jugglers 9
jumps 28, 30, 34, 35, 36, 37
Junior World Championships 42

K

Kan, Andrei 12
Kasamatsu vault 33

L

Lan, Hui 15
leaps 14, 28, 30, 35, 36
leotard 10, 11
Léotard, Jules 10
Ling, P. 10
Lisenko, Tatiana 42
Liukin, Valeri 13, 33
log roll 16
long trousers 11
lunge step 21, 22, 40, 43

M

Marinich, Vitaly 12
mats 13, 18, 22, 23, 30, 34, 40
Miller, Shannon 8, 20, 35, 42
mount 13, 28, 34, 43

O

Olympic games 12, 42
one-armed balance 38, 39

P

parallel bars 9, 12, 13
piked back somersault 41
pommel horse 12
practice beam 34, 35

R

Reeder, Annika 15
release and catch moves 13, 43
rhythmic apparatus 9, 36, 37
rhythmic gymnastics 9, 36, 37, 43
Rhythmic World Championships 42
ribbon 9, 36
rings 9, 11, 12, 13, 22
rolls 16, 17, 18, 19
Romagnoli, Travis 12
rope 9, 36, 37

round-off 24, 25, 26, 30, 31, 40, 41
run-up, vault 12

S

scoreboard 12
score box 13, 43
scoring 33, 40, 42
sequence 11, 17, 30, 31, 34, 35, 36, 37, 43
shapes 10, 14, 15, 16, 18, 20, 28, 29, 30, 32, 34, 36
shorts 10, 11
shoulder balance 39
shoulder stand balance 20
slope 18, 19
somersault 18, 26, 32, 33, 34, 40, 41, 43
spiral 37
split leap 29
splits 15, 27, 31
sports acrobatics 9, 38, 39, 40, 41, 42, 43
Sports Acrobatics World Championships 42
springboard 13, 18, 32, 34, 41
stag balance 38
stag leap 29
stamina 12, 18, 43
star jump 29
straddle lever balance 39
straddle pike jump 29
straddle sit 16
straddle stand 19
straight back somersault 41
straight leg headstand 23
strength 11, 12, 18, 30
suppleness 11, 12, 14, 15, 16
supporting 22, 23, 38
symbols 42

T

take-off 28, 32, 40
technical advisor 42, 43
tempo exercise 39, 43
top 38, 39, 43
tracksuit 11
training 8, 11, 12, 15, 18, 22
trio 39
tuck 17, 18, 19, 31, 40
tucked front somersault 18, 40, 41
tucked headstand 22
tuck jump 29
tumble run 40, 41
tumbling 9, 40, 41, 43
tumbling track 41

V

vaulting 11, 13, 22, 28, 32, 33
vaulting horse 9, 12, 13, 32, 33
voluntary exercise 30, 43
V-sit balance 20, 34

W

walkover, back 26, 27, 35, 42
wall bars 7
warm-up 11, 43
W-jump 35
World Championships 8, 12, 42
World School Games 42
World Student Games 42

Y

Y-balance 30, 34
Yurchenko vault 33

Useful addresses

Here are the addresses of some major gymnastics associations which you may find useful.

British Amateur Gymnastics Association (BAGA)
Ford Hall
Lilleshall National Sports Centre
Nr. Newport,
Shropshire TF10 9NB
England   Tel : 0952 677137

Welsh Amateur Gymnastics Association (WAGA)
Mrs S. John
Thornbury House
Thornbury Close
Rhiwibina
Cardiff CF4 1UT,
Wales

Scottish Amateur Gymnastics Association (SAGA)
8b Melville Street
Falkirk FK1 1HZ
Scotland   Tel : 0324 612308

Northern Ireland Amateur Gymnastics Association
58 Castlemore Avenue
Belfast BT6 9RG
Northern Ireland   Tel : 0222 522012

Proficiency Award Schemes
Ghyll Industrial Estate
Heathfield
East Sussex TN21 8AW
England   Tel : 0435 866210

British Schools Gymnastic Association (BSGA)
Mr. Clive Hamilton
Orchard House
15 North Common Road
Uxbridge,
Middlesex UB8 1PD
England   Tel : 0895 233377

Fédération Internationale de Gymnastique (FIG)
Rue des Oeuches 10
2740 Moutier 1
Switzerland

International Federation of Sports Acrobatics (IFSA)
18 Z. Levski Blvd.
1000 Sofia
Bulgaria

Cheryl

Lucy

Ben

Adam

Becky

Chloe

Nick

Acknowledgments

Dorling Kindersley would like to thank the following people
for their help in the production of this book:

All the Young Gymnasts for their enthusiasm and patience during the photographic sessions; Clem Malcolmson of Woking Gymnastic Club, Surrey, for providing the artistic gymnasts and the venue; and all the staff at Woking, especially Sue James, for the advice and practical assistance so willingly given; Jan and Tony Wills of the King Edmund Gym Club, Yate, Bristol for helping with the section on sports acrobatics and providing the sports acrobats; Catherine Smith of Spelthorne School of Gymnastics, Ashford, Middlesex for her guidance on rhythmic gymnastics and providing the rhythmic gymnast; Patsy Burrell of Burrell Designs, for making the leotards; and Bernadette Crowley, Linda Martin, and Susan Peach for additional editorial assistance.

Picture credits
key: B bottom; L left; R right; C centre; T top.
Allsport/Gerard Vandystadt: 33TC
Mary Evans: 9CR, 9CL
Gymnova: 10BL
Mansell: 9TL, 9TR
Felipe Sanchez Monsivais: 8BR
Sporting Pictures: 8BL, 20TR, 35TR
Supersport/Eileen Langsley: 8BC,
8TL, 12CL, 12TR, 12CR, 13CLB,
13CRB & 13T, 15TL, 15CR, 22CL,
27TR, 29BL, 33TR, 36BR

Inside jacket: Cary Garrison
(Edmond, Oklahoma, USA) TR
Back jacket: Supersport/
Eileen Langsley BR

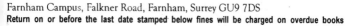

THE SURREY INSTITUTE OF ART & DESIGN
UNIVERSITY COLLEGE

63993

Farnham Campus, Falkner Road, Farnham, Surrey GU9 7DS
Return on or before the last date stamped below fines will be charged on overdue books

- 8 NOV 2000

- 3 DEC 2001

- 5 OCT 2001

- 4 MAR 2002   2 8 MAR 2003

1 3 DEC 2000

2 9 JAN 2002

- 8 JAN 2001

2 1 MAR 2002   2 3 JUN 20

29. APR

- 5 FEB 2001

1 3 MAY 2002   1 0 OCT 200

7 NOV 2003

- 1 DEC 2003

- 5 FEB 2001

2 0 JAN 2003

- 8 DEC 2003

2 1 MAR 2001

2 0 FEB 2003

- 6 MAR 2003   3 MAR 2004

2 5 MAY 2001

- 1 OCT 2004   2 0 MAR 2003

1 3 JUN 2003

2 0 JUN 2001

2 5 OCT 2001

- 7 NOV 2003

2 4 MAY 2004